The Pen

Margaret Atwood is an acclaimed novelist and poet whose many works include *The Handmaid's Tale*, *Alias Grace*, *Oryx and Crake* and *The Blind Assassin*, for which she won the Booker Prize. She is the recipient of many other prestigious awards, and her work has been translated into over thirty-five languages. She lives in Toronto.

MARGARET ATWOOD

The Penelopiad

faber and faber

First published in 2007
by Faber and Faber Limited
The Bindery, 51 Hatton Garden,
London ECIN 8HN

Typeset by Country Setting, Kingsdown, Kent CT14 8ES

Printed and bound by CPI Group (UK) Ltd, Croydon, CR0 4YY

A CIP record for this book
is available from the British Library

978-0-571-23949-8

Author's Introduction

The play you hold in your hands is an echo of an echo of an echo of an echo of an echo of an echo.

The original explosion was the Trojan War, some version of which – say the archeologists – may well have taken place at an undetermined date in the Bronze Age.

The first echo of it was the motherlode of mythic and legendary and therefore originally oral Trojan War material – fluid in nature, with different stories told in different ways in different places. The next echo was *The Odyssey*, an epic poem – or, as Robert Graves would have it, the first novel – that drew on this mythic material, but chose some versions while excluding others.

The next echo consists of the many post-Homeric retellings, stretching from Ovid through Dante and Chaucer and Shakespeare and Tennyson to James Joyce and Derek Walcott and Barry Unsworth and Lewis Hyde, with many more works by many other writers. Nor is the wellspring exhausted yet.

The next echo was my small book called *The Penelopiad*, written as part of the Canongate Myths Series, and published in over thirty languages in the fall of 2005.

The fifth echo was a forty-minute dramatised version of the first quarter of the book, presented at St James' Church, Picadilly, for one night only, at the time of the 'Myths Series' launch. This event grew out of conversations with Phyllida Lloyd concerning the dramatic possibilities of the book, and was directed by her. It was rehearsed during off-hours in a theatre bar, and then in the upstairs room of Waterstone's, Piccadilly. There were three Maids, who also played the other parts – Penelope's Naiad mother, Helen of Troy and Odysseus himself. (I read the part of Penelope on that occasion, and lived to tell the tale.)

And now, here is the sixth echo: the stage adaptation of The *Penelopiad*.

*

The Penelopiad – the book version – is not simply a re-telling of *The Odyssey*, but includes episodes drawn from the first echo – the body of mythic material not used in *The Odyssey* – such as Penelope's childhood, her marriage and the slanderous rumours about her. It was conceived as a composition for two voices – the voice of Penelope her-self, and the collective voice of the twelve maids – or slaves – who are hanged at the end of *The Odyssey*. The hanging of these maids bothered me when I first read *The Odyssey* as a teenager, and it bothers me still, as it is so excessive in relation to anything they actually did.

Both voices – that of Penelope and that of the Maids – speak from the Greek Underworld, where Penelope is free to tell the story from her point of view. Many events that stretch credulity in *The Odyssey* (would Penelope really not have recognised Odysseus when he turns up disguised as a beggar? Would she not have noticed when Odysseus almost strangles Eurycleia?) are best explained by wilful silence on the part of Penelope, or by motives not explored in *The Odyssey*, though the possibilities for them can be found in it.

The chorus of Maids is in part a tribute to the use of the chorus in Greek tragedy, in which lowly characters comment on the main action, and also to the satyr plays that accom-panied tragedies, in which comic actors made fun of them. The Maids in *The Penelopiad* do such things, but also they're angry, as they still feel they have been wrongfully hanged.

It was this choral activity that suggested the idea of having the Maids play both themselves and also all the other characters in the drama except Penelope. Although in this initial production we are lucky to have the full complement of twelve Maids, the play could be done with as few as seven – all female, mixed, or even all male. In this respect, the play retains the fluidity of the original mythic material.

As to the main characters: Penelope herself – although somewhat weepy – is resourceful and brave, and (as befits the wife of Odyseus, master trickster) a good liar. Some have made a comparison with *Desperate Housewives*, but that's a case of convergence, because Penelope is perhaps the first desperate housewife to appear in art. (Absent husband, teenage son giving lip and breaking curfew, louts gobbling up the foodstuffs, a servant problem – who wouldn't be desperate?)

Odysseus is a famous hero – but by *hero* the Greeks did not mean a Superman-like creature who always behaves well. He was known to the ancients as a shifty fellow – a charming smooth-talker and inventor of crafty dodges, who shaped himself to circumstance. I have tried to do justice to these attributes.

Telemachus is an adolescent boy raised in a household of doting females who is then confronted by a hundred and twenty challengers. No wonder he's surly.

*

The structure of *The Penelopiad* – the book version – owes something to the scrapbook or sampler, and as such has numerous digressions. The interruptions of the Maids represent many forms, from ballad to Tennysonian Idyll. Sadly, in the dramatic adaptation we've had to cut some of these digressions: the eighteenth-century playlet, the Gravesian lecture – for length, and because they conflicted with the forward thrust of the play. Of 'The Trial of Odysseus', in which the evidence for and against the hanging of the

Maids is set forth, nothing remains but the Invocation to the Furies.

It would be possible to envisage a different adaptation, in which these and other scenes would be preserved. The ancient myths remain fertile ground. Who knows what might sprout from them next?

AUTHOR'S THANKS

Every play is a palimpsest, composed of many layers of writing and suggestion; and every play is shaped by the circumstances of its development. Many people have been involved in this one.

First thanks to Jamie Byng of Canongate, who tangled me in the web of the 'Myths Series', to Vivienne Schuster and Louise Dennys of Knopf Canada, who did the primary editing of the book, from which so much of the text in the play has come.

I'd next like to thank Phyllida Lloyd, and all those others who participated in the first *Penelopiad* one-night stand. These included Heather Craney, Rebecca Jenkins and Kim Medcalf as the Maids; Kieron Docherty, who was Production Manager; Anthony Van Last, who was Movement Director; and Jason Carr, who composed the original music. Erica Wagner and the *Sunday Times* must be thanked for their financial and moral support, as must Peter Florence of the Hay-on-Wye Festival.

For this production, I'd like to thank Peter Hinton of the National Arts Centre in Ottawa, who first commissioned the adaptation, and Deborah Shaw of the Royal Shakespeare Company, who agreed to this unprecedented co-production; and Joe Phillips of Curtis Brown, who was my agent for this play.

I'd next like to thank the 'Group of Seven' – the seven remarkable Canadian women donors who made this production possible: Gail Asper, Alice Burton, Zita Cobb, Kiki Delaney, Julia Foster, Leslie Gales and Gail O'Brien.

In the next instance, much thanks is due to Jeanie O'Hare, the dedicated Literary Manager of the RSC, who plunged in with both hands, and to the indefatigable Nicola Wilson, who in her role as dramaturg initially suggested how the scenes might flow, and then hovered over the play-script like Eurycleia over Telemachus.

The electric director, Josette Bushell-Mingo, made many helpful suggestions about the script, as did the perceptive leading lady, Penny Downie. For the visual aspects of the play, Veronica Tennant as Movement Director, Bonnie Beecher as Lighting Designer, and Rosa Maggiora as Designer were indispensable. The amazing music and sounds were composed by Warren Wills.

Finally, I must thank the twelve supremely talented actresses who played the extremely demanding roles of the Maids: Mojisola Adebayo, Jade Anouka, Lisa Karen Cox, Derbhle Crotty, Philippa Domville, Kate Hennig, Pauline Hutton, Corinne Koslo, Sarah Malin, Pamela Matthews, Kelly McIntosh and Jenny Young.

For without the Maids, there would be no *Penelopiad*.

Margaret Atwood, 2007

The Penelopiad was first performed by the Royal Shakespeare Company in association with Canada's National Arts Centre at The Swan Theatre, Stratford-upon-Avon, on 27 July 2007. The cast was as follows:

Telemachus/Maid Mojisola Adebayo
Melantho of the Pretty Cheeks/Maid 1 Jade Anouka
Antinous/Maid/Suitor 1 Derbhle Crotty
Maid 2 Lisa Karen Cox
Naiad Mother/Maid Philippa Domville
Penelope Penny Downie
Eurycleia/Maid Kate Hennig
Oracle/Maid 3 Pauline Hutton
Icarius/Maid/Suitor 2 Corrine Koslo
Odysseus/Maid Sarah Malin
Laertes/Suitor 3/Maid Pamela Matthews
Helen/Maid Kelly McIntosh
Anticleia/Maid 4 Jenny Young

Directed by Josette Bushell-Mingo
Designed by Rosa Maggiora
Lighting designed by Bonnie Beecher
Dramaturg Nicola Wilson
Music by Warren Wills
Sound designed by Martin Slavin
Movement Director Veronica Tennant
Fights by Alison de Burgh
Assistant Director Rae Mcken
Music Director Michael Cryne
Company Voice Work by Charmian Gradwell
Casting by Sam Jones CDG
Production Manager Rebecca Watts
Costume Supervisor Christine Rowland
Company Manager Jondon
Stage Manager Janet Gautrey
Deputy Stage Manager Gabrielle Sanders
Assistant Stage Manager Sally Hughes

Characters

Penelope
Odysseus
Telemachus
Helen of Troy
Menelaus
Penelope's Naiad Mother
King Icarius of Sparta
Oracle
Eurycleia
Laertes, King of Ithaca
Anticleia, Queen of Ithaca
Antinous
Appolonius

THE MAIDS

Melantho
Tanis
Kerthia
Iole
Celandine
Klytie
Selene
Zoe
Alecto
Chloris
Phasiana
Narcissa

COSTUME DESIGNS

Rosa Maggiora

Penelope

fine pleating
below knee

MAID

RM2007

Maid

brocade matador style
breast plate

Odysseus

Telemachus

Naiad Mother

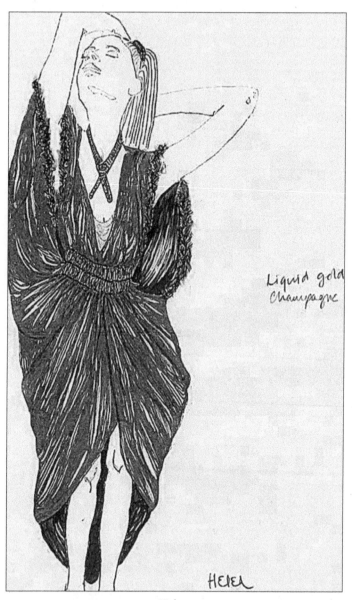

Liquid gold
Champagne

HELEN

Helen

THE PENELOPIAD

Act One

Hades.

Penelope

Now that I'm dead I know everything. This is what
I wished would happen, but like so many of my
wishes it's failed to come true. I know only a few
factoids that I didn't know before. Death is much too
high a price to pay for the satisfaction of curiosity,
needless to say.

Since being dead – since achieving this state of
bonelessness, liplessness, breastlessness – I've learned
some things I would rather not know, as one does
when listening at windows or opening other people's
letters. You think you'd like to read minds? Think
again.

Down here everyone arrives with a sack, like the sacks
used to keep the winds in, but each of these sacks is
full of words – words you've spoken, words you've
heard, words that have been said about you. Some
sacks are very small, others large; my own is of a
reasonable size, though a lot of the words in it concern
my eminent husband. What a fool he made of me,
some say. It was a specialty of his: making fools. He
got away with everything, which was another of his
specialties: getting away.

He was always so plausible. Many people believed
that his version of events was the true one, give
or take a few murders, a few beautiful seductresses,

3

a few one-eyed monsters. But I like to think he never played his tricks on me. For hadn't I been faithful? Didn't I wait, and wait, and wait, despite the temptation – almost the compulsion – to do otherwise? And yet what have I amounted to, now the official version has gained ground? An edifying legend. A stick used to beat other women with. Why can't they be as considerate, as trustworthy, as all-suffering as I was? That's the line they take, the singers, the yarn-spinners. *Don't follow my example*, I want to scream in your ears – yes, yours! But when I try to scream, I sound like an owl.

SCENE 2
A ROPE-JUMPING RHYME

Hades.

The Maids interrupt Penelope. They dance in, each holding a rope.

Maids (*while jumping ropes, or doing other rope tricks*)
we are the maids
the ones you killed
the ones you failed

we danced in air
our bare feet twitched
it was not fair

with every goddess, queen and bitch
from there to here
you scratched your itch

we did much less
than what you did
you judged us bad

4

you had the spear
you had the word
at your command

we scrubbed the blood
of our dead par-
amours from floors, from chairs

from stairs, from doors
we knelt in water
while you stared

at our bare feet
it was not fair
you licked our fear

it gave you pleasure
you raised your hand
you watched us fall

we danced on air
the ones you failed
the ones you killed

Penelope

I turned a blind eye, back then, when I was alive.
I didn't ask awkward questions, I didn't dig deep.
I wanted happy endings. And happy endings are best
achieved by keeping your mouth shut, and the right
doors locked.

After I was dead, they turned me into a story; though
not the kind of story I would have preferred to hear.
I waited. I waited some more. Now that all the others
have run out of air, it's my turn. Once, people would
have laughed if I'd tried to play the minstrel – there's
nothing more preposterous than an aristocrat fumbling
around with the arts – but who cares about public
opinion now? The opinion of shadows, of echoes. So
I'll spin a thread of my own.

SCENE 3
PENELOPE'S CHILDHOOD

Penelope

Where shall I begin? My father was King Icarius of
Sparta.

He appears.

My mother was a Naiad.

She appears.

Daughters of Naiads were a dime a dozen in those
days; the place was crawling with them. Nevertheless,
it never hurts to be of semi-divine birth. Or it never
hurts immediately.

*The adult Penelope observes the following scene.
King Icarius is consulting the Oracle. She has a
snake/rope draped around her; its head is whispering
into her ear.*

Icarius

What's it saying?

*The Oracle consults the snake, reacts with alarm to its
message.*

Oracle

You have a very young child. A daughter.

Icarius

Yes?

Oracle

The gods have given her intelligence, and a faithful
and patient nature.

6

Icarius
Good.

Oracle
She will weave her father's shroud.

Icarius
Her father's shroud?

Oracle
Father, father-in-law . . . something with father in it.

Icarius
She'll *kill* me?

Oracle
It's not totally clear. The gods often mumble.

Icarius
She'll kill *me*?

Oracle
The Divine Snake has spoken.

The Oracle leaves.

Icarius
Bring Penelope!

A bundled Penelope is carried out.

Throw her into the sea!

His Servants hesitate.

Maid
But she's only a child!

Icarius
Do as I say! Drown her!

The Penelope bundle is thrown into the sea. Icarius hides his face in sorrow.

7

Penelope

Luckily, a flock of purple-striped ducks came to my rescue, and towed me ashore.

A dozen ducks come to her rescue. They tow the Penelope bundle to shore, and stand around her, quacking.

Icarius

What's all this noise? Purple-striped ducks?
It must be an omen.

The ducks fly away to reveal the beached Penelope.

Icarius (*picking up the bundle*)

She lives! My duckie lives! The gods have spoken!

Penelope

And so I became known as Duckie.

Perhaps I have only invented the oracle story in order to make myself feel better. So much whispering goes on here, in the dark caverns, in the meadows, that sometimes it's hard to know whether the whispering is coming from others or from the inside of your own head. I use *head* figuratively. We have dispensed with heads, as such, down here.

But it was stupid of Icarius to try to drown the daughter of a Naiad. Water is our element, it is our birthright. Although we are not such good swimmers as our mothers, we do have a way of floating, and we're well-connected among the fish and seabirds.

My mother, like all Naiads, was beautiful, but chilly at heart. She had waving hair and dimples, and rippling laughter. She was elusive. When I was little I often tried to throw my arms around her, but she had a habit of sliding away.

I like to think that she may have been responsible for calling up that flock of ducks, but probably she wasn't: she preferred swimming in the river to the care of small children, and I often slipped her mind. If my father hadn't had me thrown into the sea she might have dropped me in herself, in a fit of absent-mindedness or irritation. She had a short attention span and rapidly changing emotions. Have I forgotten to tell you she had rather small pointed teeth?

Being thrown into the sea did not improve my relations with my father. There I would be, strolling hand in hand with my apparently fond male parent along a cliff edge or a river bank or a parapet, and the thought would occur to me that he might suddenly decide to shove me over or bash me to death with a rock.

It is to this episode that I attribute my reserve, as well as my mistrust of other people's intentions. I was a child who learned early the virtues of self-sufficiency. I knew that I would have to look out for myself in the world. I could hardly count on family support.

SCENE 4
CHORUS: KIDDIE MOURN, A LAMENT

Maids

We too were children. We too were born to the wrong parents. Poor parents, slave parents, peasant parents, and serf parents; parents who sold us, parents from whom we were stolen. These parents were not gods, they were not demi-gods, they were not nymphs or Naiads. We were set to work in the palace, as children; we drudged from dawn to dusk, as children. If we wept, no one dried our tears. If we slept, we

9

were kicked awake. We were told we were motherless. We were told we were fatherless. We were told we were lazy. We were told we were dirty. We were dirty. Dirt was our concern, dirt was our business, dirt was our specialty, dirt was our fault. We were the dirty girls. If our owners or the sons of our owners or a visiting nobleman or the sons of a visiting nobleman wanted to sleep with us, we could not refuse. It did us no good to weep, it did us no good to say we were in pain. All this happened to us when we were children. If we were pretty children our lives were worse. We ground the flour for lavish wedding feasts, then we ate the leftovers; we would never have a wedding feast of our own, no rich gifts would be exchanged for us; our bodies had little value. But we wanted to sing and dance too, we wanted to be happy too. As we grew older we became polished and evasive, we mastered the secret sneer. We swayed our hips, we lurked, we winked, we signalled with our eyebrows, even when we were children; we met boys behind the pig pens, noble boys and ignoble boys alike. We rolled around in the straw, in the mud, in the dung, on the beds of soft fleece we were making up for our masters. We drank the wine left in the wine cups. We spat onto the serving platters. Between the bright hall and the dark scullery we crammed filched meat into our mouths. We laughed together in our attics, in our nights. We snatched what we could.

SCENE 5
THE LAND OF ASPHODEL

Hades.

Penelope

It's dark here, many have remarked. Dark Death, they
say – or the gloomy halls of Hades. This is true, but
one can always take a walk through the fields of
asphodel. It's brighter there, and a certain amount
of vapid dancing goes on, though the region sounds
better than it is. The fields of asphodel has a poetic lilt
to it, but while the white flowers are pretty enough, a
person soon gets tired of them. I would have preferred
an assortment of colours, a few winding paths and
vistas and stone benches and fountains, perhaps the
odd hyacinth or a sprinkling of crocuses. Though we
never get spring here, or any other seasons for that
matter. But I shouldn't complain.

Every once in a while the fogs part and we get a
glimpse of the world of the living. It's like rubbing
the glass on a dirty window, making a space to look
through. Sometimes the barrier dissolves and we can
go on an outing. Then we get very excited, and there
is a great deal of squeaking.

The difficulty, of course, is that I have no mouth
through which I can speak. I can't make myself
understood, not in your world, the world of bodies,
of tongues and fingers; and most of the time I have
no listeners, not on your side of the river. Those of
you who may catch the odd whisper, the odd squeak,
so easily mistake my words for breezes rustling the
dry reeds, for bats at twilight, for bad dreams.

But I've always been of a determined nature. Patient, they used to call me. I like to see a thing through to the end.

SCENE 6
PENELOPE'S MARRIAGE

The Palace Courtyard. Penelope and her Maids are upstairs. The men assemble downstairs.

Penelope
My marriage was arranged.

Four Maids dress Penelope. The Maids address the audience.

Spartan Maid 1
Marriages are for having children.

Spartan Maid 2
And children are not toys and pets.

Spartan Maid 3
Children are vehicles for passing things along.

Spartan Maid 2
Kingdoms.

Spartan Maid 4
Wedding gifts.

Spartan Maid 1
Loot!

Spartan Maid 3
Stories.

Spartan Maid 2
Grudges.

Spartan Maid 1
Through children, alliances are forged.

Spartan Maid 2
Through children, wrongs are avenged.

Spartan Maid 4
To have a child is to set loose a force in the world.

Spartan Maid 3
And if you have an enemy it is best to kill his sons.

Spartan Maid 2
For as long as they're alive, they are a danger to you.

King Icarius is downstairs putting together the rich dowry.

Icarius
If you have daughters instead of sons, you need to get them married off as soon as possible so you can have grandsons. The more sword-wielders and spear-throwers you can count on within your own family, the better.

In my court we honour the ancient custom of holding an athletic contest to determine a suitable match. And so whoever wins the foot race wins my daughter's hand in marriage, and a substantial dowry.

A crowd of Suitors gathers in the courtyard, Odysseus among them.

Odysseus
So, my fellow noblemen. Drinks before the race?

Suitor 1
The drinks will be in my honour afterwards, you can count on that!

Suitor 3 (*to Suitor 2*)
You're not running in *those* sandals!

Suitor 1 (*to Suitor 3*)
Appolonius! You've put on weight! Eating well?

Odysseus pours water for all the Suitors.

Suitor (*composing a song with his lute*)
Penelope, I love you madly!
For you – I'd give my life so gladly!
Thy beauteous nose
Is like a rose . . .

*The Suitors look at him and laugh at him. Odysseus
spikes the drinks.*

Odysseus
It's a hot day. Drink up!

Upstairs, looking down.

Penelope
Who's the barrel-chested one?

Spartan Maid 1
Oh, that's only Odysseus.

Spartan Maid 2
From Ithaca.

Penelope
Ithaca?

Spartan Maid 3
Some god-forsaken goat-strewn rock.

Spartan Maid 4
What *is* he wearing?

Spartan Maid 3
He looks like a goatherd.

Spartan Maid 2
And a cheat and a thief.

Spartan Maid 4
Just like his grandfather, Autolycus.

Spartan Maid 1
They say he's very clever, though.

Spartan Maid 3
Too clever for his own good.

Penelope
I wonder how fast he can run.

Spartan Maid 1
Not very fast, on those short legs of his!

Penelope
Maybe his legs only *seem* short because we're looking down at him.

Spartan Maid 3
He'll tell you the size – of his legs – doesn't matter.

Spartan Maid 1
But you know what they say about short legs!

Penelope
What?

Spartan Maid 1 wiggles her little finger.

Tiny fingers?

Penelope doesn't get the joke. The Maids laugh at her.

Spartan Maid 1
Aww. Bless her. She's only a kid.

Spartan Maid 4
So he'll know just how to deal with her!

Spartan Maid 3
She'll be bleating soon enough!

Spartan Maid 1
Like a goat to the slaughter!

Spartan Maid 2
It really hurts!

Spartan Maid 4
Like your insides have been torn apart!

Spartan Maid 1
You'll cry!

Spartan Maid 2
You'll scream!

Spartan Maid 4
You'll bleed!

Spartan Maid 3
You'll beg . . .

Spartan Maid 1
For more!

Maids laugh. Penelope is frightened.

Helen enters.

Helen
What's the big joke?

Spartan Maid 1
Princess Helen!

Spartan Maid 2
We were just talking about Odysseus, my lady.

Helen
Indeed! I think Odysseus would make a very suitable husband for our little duckie. She likes the quiet life,

after all. And she'll certainly have that if he takes her to Ithaca, as he's boasting of doing.

She glances at Penelope, sighs.

You could help him look after his goats. I think you'd look quite sweet together. You both have such short legs.

The Maids snigger. Penelope looks down at her legs.

Never mind, little cousin. They say he's very clever. And you're very clever too, they tell me. So at least you'll be able to understand what he says. I certainly never could! It's lucky for both of us that he didn't win *me*!

Helen exits to rejoin the main group, leaving Penelope discouraged.

Music. The company – all except Penelope and her Maids, who remain upstairs – gather to watch the race.

Penelope's Naiad Mother wafts in, dressed in blue, a puddle gathering at her feet. A Maid mops up behind her.

Icarius
Noblemen. On your marks!

Spartan Maid 2
They're all looking at Helen!

Spartan Maid 4
She knows how to melt their knees.

Icarius
Get set!

Spartan Maid 1
Her husband looks furious.

17

Spartan Maid 2
Menelaus. He's so loud.

Spartan Maid 4
But he's so rich!

A gong. The men run off. The Maids watch.

Spartan Maid 3
Ooh!

Spartan Maid 2
They're running well.

Spartan Maid 1
But they're slowing down on the far side.

Spartan Maid 4
They're *really* slowing down.

Spartan Maid 2
What's happening?

Spartan Maid 3
Odysseus is going strong!

Spartan Maid 4
He's overtaking!

Spartan Maid 2
He's in the lead!

Spartan Maid 1
The gods have favoured . . . Odysseus?

Odysseus enters in triumph. The other Suitors are crestfallen. Muted congratulations. Icarius looks annoyed.

Spartan Maid 3
Princess Penelope . . . time for your wedding.

The Maids cover Penelope's face with a veil and escort her downstairs to join Odysseus. Solemn festivities.

Penelope
I had trouble making it through the ceremony – the sacrifices of animals, the offerings to the gods, the lustral sprinklings, the libations, the prayers, the interminable songs. I felt quite dizzy. I kept my eyes downcast, so all I could see of Odysseus was the lower part of his body. Short legs, I kept thinking, even at the most solemn moments. This was not an appropriate thought – it was trivial and silly, and it made me want to giggle – but in my own defence I must point out that I was only fifteen.

And so I was handed over to Odysseus, like a package of meat. A sort of gilded blood pudding.

The Maids fuss over Penelope's costume while the wedding feast is being brought on. Her Naiad Mother interrupts.

Naiad Mother
Penelope, my child.

Penelope curtsies.

Penelope
Yes, Mother.

Naiad Mother
Remember this – water does not resist. Water flows. When you plunge your hand into it, all you feel is a caress. For water is not a solid wall, and will not stop you. Water always goes where it wants to go, and nothing in the end can stand against it. Water is patient. Dripping water wears away a stone. Remember that, my child. Remember you are half water. If you can't go through an obstacle, go around it. Water does.

*The company take their seats. They are served hunks of
bread and meat on platters; they eat with their hands.
Wine, music and frivolity. All the men are magnetised
by Helen, except Icarius, who is getting drunk.*

Odysseus
A toast to my wife. The fair and intelligent Penelope!

All
The fair and intelligent Penelope!

*They all drink. Icarius bangs his cup on the table
angrily.*

*The men – including Odysseus – are still transfixed by
Helen.*

Penelope (*aside*)
Your cup is empty, Sir. May I fill it?

Odysseus (*still looking at Helen*)
If a man lives by his wits, as I do, he needs to have
those wits always at hand and kept sharp, like axes
or swords. Only fools are given to bragging about
how much they can drink.

*He tears a piece of meat in two and hands half to
Penelope, still looking at Helen.*

Icarius
He cheated! Short legs! Nothing but goats! All he
wants is my gold. My golden duckie. He's taking her
away!

Penelope
I couldn't eat a thing. I was too nervous. I was certain
Odysseus would be disappointed in me once he made
his way in through the shimmering robe. But he
wasn't looking at me, and neither was anyone else.

They were all staring at Helen, who was intolerably beautiful, as usual. Like every other man on earth, Odysseus had desperately wanted to win her hand. I was at best only second prize. And although mine was the marriage in question, Helen wanted all the attention for herself. I suspect she used to flirt with her dog, with her mirror, with her comb, with her bedpost. She needed to keep in practice.

But in a way it was lucky that she was distracting everyone's attention, because it kept them from noticing me and my trembling and awkwardness. I wasn't just nervous. I was terrified.

SCENE 7
THE WEDDING NIGHT

Odysseus and Penelope are led to the bridal chamber.

The Maids garland the bed and sprinkle the threshold. Vulgar jokes and drunken yelling from the men. Odysseus laughs loudly. The procession leaves. Odysseus bolts the door. Banging and shouting from outside. Penelope is shaking.

Odysseus
Come over here.

Penelope approaches.

Forget everything you've been told. I'm not going to hurt you, or not very much. But it would help us both if you could pretend. I've been told you're a clever girl. Do you think you could manage a few screams? That'll satisfy them – they're listening at the door – and then they'll leave us in peace and we can take our time to become friends.

Odysseus smiles. Penelope smiles back, then starts
screaming. The crowd outside cheer and then depart.
Odysseus and Penelope laugh. He kisses her, caresses
her gently, and starts unpinning her robe.

Penelope

I knew the fiction was that the bride had to be stolen.
The consummation of a marriage was supposed to be
a sanctioned rape. A conquest, a trampling of a foe,
a mock killing. There was supposed to be blood.

But this was one of Odysseus' great secrets as a
persuader – he could convince anyone that together
they faced a common obstacle, and only together
could they overcome it. He could draw almost any
listener into a collaboration, a little conspiracy of his
own making. Nobody could do this better than he:
for once, the stories don't lie.

Somewhat later I found that Odysseus was not one
of those men who, after the act, simply roll over and
begin to snore. No, Odysseus wanted to talk, and
as he was an excellent raconteur I was happy to listen.
I think this is what he valued most in me: my ability
to appreciate his stories. It's an underrated talent, in
women.

He told me many stories – stories about his exploits
and his looting expeditions, and how he'd always
been favoured by the goddess Athene because of his
inventive mind and his skill at disguises.

He showed me the long scar on his thigh, and told me
how he came by it – he'd been savaged by a ferocious
boar while hunting – and how after a tremendous
battle he'd killed the boar! He told me about his special
bow that nobody but he could string, and how he could

shoot an arrow through twelve round axe-heads – an astonishing feat! In return, I told him the story of my own near-drowning. He said that he himself would never think of drowning such a precious girl as me.

By the time the morning came, I found I'd developed friendly feelings towards Odysseus – more than that, loving and passionate feelings – and he behaved as if he reciprocated them.

And so when, a few days later, he announced his intention of taking me and my dowry back with him to Ithaca, I was only too pleased to go.

SCENE 8
SAILING TO ITHACA

CHORUS: SONG – IF I WAS A PRINCESS

Maid 1
If I was a princess, with silver and gold,
And loved by a hero, I'd never grow old:
Oh, if a young hero came a-marrying me,
I'd always be beautiful, happy, and free!

Chorus
Then sail, my fine lady, on the billowing wave –
The water below is as dark as the grave,
And maybe you'll sink in your little blue boat –
It's hope, and hope only, that keeps us afloat.

Maid 2
I fetch and I carry, I hear and obey.
It's 'Yes sir' and 'No ma'am' the whole bleeding day;
I smile and I nod with a tear in my eye,
I make the soft beds in which others do lie.

Maid 3

    O gods and O prophets, please alter my life,
    And let a young hero take me for his wife!
    But no hero comes to me, early or late –
    Hard work is my destiny, death is my fate!

Chorus

    Then sail, my fine lady, on the billowing wave –
    The water below is as dark as the grave,
    And maybe you'll sink in your little blue boat –
    It's hope, and hope only, that keeps us afloat.

SCENE 9
WELCOME TO ITHACA

*The Maids can perform the sea voyage during the
following account by Penelope.*

Penelope

    The sea voyage to Ithaca was long and frightening.
    I spent most of the time lying down or throwing up.
    Meanwhile, Odysseus was either at the bow, peering
    ahead to spot rocks and sea serpents and other dangers,
    or at the tiller, directing the ship.

    I'd gained a great opinion of Odysseus since our
    wedding day, and I admired him immensely.

    As we drew closer, I saw that the harbour at Ithaca was
    surrounded by steep, rocky cliffs, thickly sprinkled
    with goats.

    The crew start cheering.

Sailor

    Ithaca! Ithaca!

Odysseus

    Drop the sails! Prepare to land!

*The jubilant court of Ithaca assembles on the shore
to greet them. Penelope and Odysseus disembark. The
Sailors carry ashore Penelope's gold dowry, in buckets.
The onlookers are in thrall to her loot.*

Odysseus (*to Penelope*)
This is my father, King Laertes, and my mother,
Queen Anticleia.

Penelope curtsies. Anticleia smiles dismissively.

Mother, Father . . . may I present my wife, Penelope,
Princess of Sparta, future Queen of Ithaca, and cousin
to the famous Helen.

Laertes (*taking her hand*)
Welcome, Princess Penelope. I trust you will be very
happy here.

Anticleia gives a frosty nod.

Anticleia
Yes, yes.
(*Aside to Odysseus.*) She's certainly very *young*.

Odysseus
A fault that will correct itself in time.

Anticleia
Very young. And sickly looking. I fear she won't live
long.

Odysseus
Penelope, this is my beloved old nurse, Eurycleia. She's
been in the house ever since my father bought her
thirty years ago.

Eurycleia (*to Penelope*)
And his father never laid a finger on me. Imagine that!
And I was very good-looking in those days! But he
always respected me greatly.

Ithacan Maid 1 (*behind her back, to Tanis*)
It wasn't respect. He was afraid of his wife!

Ithacan Maid 2
That Anticleia would freeze the balls off Helios.

Eurycleia (*to Odysseus*)
Beloved Master. I'm overjoyed that you have returned safely. I've kept everything just as you wanted it.

She kneels, kisses his hand.

Odysseus
I can always depend on *you*.

Eurycleia
Now, girls! Back to your chores!

(*To Penelope.*) You just come along with me, my dear. I'm the one to show you how things are done here in Ithaca. And nobody knows Odysseus the way I do, for didn't I nurse him as a baby and bring him up as a youth, and tend to that awful wound on his thigh that he got from the wild boar that time? He's still got the scar! But I'm sure you've seen it! I know exactly how he likes his things – his breakfast, his bath, his robes, well, every little detail.

You should just leave all that to me! We've got to fatten you up so you can have a nice big son for Odysseus! That's *your* job!

CHORUS: THE BIRTH OF TELEMACHUS
AN IDYLL

Chorus

    Nine months he sailed the wine-red seas of his
        mother's blood
    Out of the cave of dreaded Night, of sleep,
    Of troubling dreams he sailed
    In his frail dark boat, the boat of himself,
    Through the dangerous ocean of his vast mother he
        sailed
    From the distant cave where the threads of men's lives
        are spun,
    Then measured, and then cut short
    By the Three Fatal Sisters, intent on their gruesome
        handcrafts,
    And the lives of women also are twisted into the
        strand.

    And we, the twelve who were later to die by his hand
    At his father's relentless command,
    Sailed as well, in the dark frail boats of ourselves
    Through the turbulent seas of our swollen and sore-
        footed mothers
    Who were not royal queens, but a motley and piebald
        collection,
    Bought, traded, captured, kidnapped from serfs and
        strangers.

    After the nine-month voyage we came to shore,
    Beached at the same time as he was, struck by the
        hostile air,
    Infants when he was an infant, wailing just as he
        wailed,

Helpless as he was helpless, but ten times more
    helpless as well,
But his birth was longed-for and feasted, as our births
    were not.

[We were his pets and his toythings, mock sisters, his
    tiny companions.
We grew as he grew, laughed also, ran as he ran,
Though sandier, hungrier, sun-speckled, most days
    meatless.
He saw us as rightfully his, for whatever purpose
He chose, to tend him and feed him, to wash him,
    amuse him,
Rock him to sleep in the dangerous boats of ourselves.]
[*Optional.*]

If we had known what the Fates knew, would we have
    drowned him back then?
Twelve against one, he wouldn't have stood a chance.
Would we? In only a minute, when nobody else was
    looking?
Pushed his still-innocent child's head under the water
With our own still-innocent childish nursemaid hands,
And blamed it on waves. Would we have had it in us?
Ask the Three Sisters, spinning their blood-red mazes,
Tangling the lives of men and women together.
Only they know our hearts.
From us you will get no answer.

*We hear the screams of Penelope in labour, followed
by a baby crying. Lights up on Odysseus and Penelope
smiling over their newborn child. The moment is
quickly interrupted:*

Eurycleia (*snatching the baby from Penelope's arms*)
    Just look! A perfect little prince! Uzzy woo! A google
    woogle poo! You lie down, child. I'll take over now.

28

Odysseus
I'm proud of you, my little duck. Even Helen hasn't
borne a son, yet.

Penelope (*smiling through gritted teeth*)
Why was he always thinking about Helen?

Odysseus and Eurycleia leave with baby Telemachus.

SCENE 11
HOME LIFE AT THE PALACE

Penelope
I had little authority in my new home. Eurycleia and
my mother-in-law ran all domestic matters. Odysseus
controlled the kingdom, naturally, with his father,
Laertes, sticking his oar in from time to time . . . It
was the standard family push-and-pull over whose
word was to carry the most weight. All were agreed
on one thing, however: it wasn't mine.

*Laertes, Anticleia, Penelope and Odysseus take their
places at the table. Eurycleia is bathing Odysseus' feet.*

Good evening, ma'am.

*Anticleia acknowledges her with a nod. The men eat
quickly.*

It's been very windy today.

Anticleia
Every day is windy, in Ithaca.

Silence.

Penelope
I went for a walk along the cliffs.

Anticleia
I hope she was accompanied.

Odysseus
Mother – she's always accompanied, you know that.

Anticleia
A king's wife is under constant scrutiny.

They eat in silence.

Laertes
One of the goats has had triplets.

Odysseus
I know.

Laertes
We'll have to eat the third one. She won't nurse it.

Odysseus
I know.

Laertes
And the pear trees need pruning.

Eurycleia
Odysseus is often too busy for domestic chores, sir.
People travel far and wide to seek his advice. He's
famous for solving problems.

Odysseus
My father doesn't approve of my . . . problem-solving.

Anticleia
Eurycleia, how is my grandson?

Eurycleia
He's thriving, my lady. He said his first word today!

Penelope
He did?

Eurycleia (*imitating*)
He said Ma-ma! He said it to *me*!

Telemachus starts crying, offstage.

He's calling me now!

Penelope gets up.

I'll go. You're barely more than a child yourself! I'll tend the little darling. You stay here and enjoy yourself!

Eurycleia leaves.

Penelope
But I did not know how to do that. My days in the palace were very lonely. I had no friend of my own age and station and very little to occupy myself with. Sometimes I would sit in the courtyard, twisting wool into thread and listening to the maids talking as they went about their chores. When it was raining I would take up my weaving in the women's quarters. There at least I would have company, as a number of slaves were always at work on the looms. And I enjoyed weaving, up to a point. It was slow and rhythmical and soothing, and nobody, even my mother-in-law, could accuse me of sitting idle while I was doing it.

But my days were mostly spent in anticipation of evenings – evenings in bed with Odysseus.

The bedroom.

Odysseus
Have I told you the secret about this bed?

Penelope
I love to hear secrets.

Odysseus

This is a very, very special bed. This bedpost here – I whittled it by hand from an olive tree with its roots still in the ground. No one will ever be able to move or displace this bed. If word gets around about the secret of my post, I'll know you've been sleeping with some other man, and then – and then – (*teasing*) I will be very cross indeed, and I'll have to chop you into little pieces with my sword.

Penelope (*laughing*)

I would never, never think of betraying your great big post.

Odysseus

Good girl. Because I'd find you out! Everyone has a hidden door, a way into their heart, and it's my special gift to be able to open it. And he who can master the hearts of men is well on the way to mastering the Fates, and controlling the thread of his own destiny.

Penelope

Do I have a hidden door into my heart? And have you found it?

Odysseus

That is for *you* to tell *me*.

Penelope

And what about the door into *your* heart? Have I found the key to that?

Odysseus smiles. He draws her closer. A shout offstage from an approaching ship. Odysseus lets go of Penelope and looks out of the window.

Odysseus

A ship – it's not one I know.

Penelope
Are you expecting news?

Odysseus
I'm always expecting news.

Odysseus takes up his cloak, and exits calmly.

SCENE 12
HELEN RUINS PENELOPE'S LIFE

Penelope
Everyone was talking about it down at the harbour. Helen of Sparta, my married cousin Helen, had run away with Paris of Troy. Paris was the younger son of King Priam and was known to be very good-looking. Apparently it was love at first sight. For nine days of feasting – laid on by Menelaus – Paris and Helen had made moon eyes at each other behind the back of Menelaus, who hadn't noticed a thing. That didn't surprise me, because the man was thick as a brick and had the manners of a stump. No doubt he hadn't stroked Helen's vanity enough, so she was ripe for someone who would. Then, when Menelaus had to go away on a trip, the two of them loaded up Paris' ship with as much gold and silver as they could carry, and eloped together.

Odysseus enters, followed by Eurycleia, and starts throwing things into a trunk.

Eurycleia
Let me do that.

Odysseus
Leave us.

Eurycleia resentfully takes her leave.

Penelope
Odysseus? What's happened? What are you doing? Where are you going?

Odysseus
I have to go to Troy.

Penelope
Troy? Why?

Odysseus
I've sworn an oath.

Penelope
What oath?

Odysseus
An oath concerning the husband of Helen. Every man who swore it will now be called on to defend the rights of Menelaus, and sail off to Troy, and wage war to get Helen back.

Penelope
But surely you don't *have* to go?

Odysseus
I swore the oath. In fact, the oath was my idea in the first place.

Penelope
What about me?

Odysseus
An oracle decreed that Troy cannot be saved without my help.

Penelope
But what about your son?

Odysseus
You must be brave. You'll have to be clever, too.

Odysseus kisses her and leaves.

Penelope

Helen! Wicked cousin Helen. Helen the lovely, Helen the irresistible, Helen the septic bitch, root of all my misfortunes. Helen should have been kept in a locked trunk in a dark cellar because she was poison on legs. Then everything would have been *fine*!

SCENE 13
TIME PASSES

Hades.

Penelope

What can I tell you about the next ten years? Odysseus sailed away to Troy. I stayed in Ithaca. The sun rose, travelled across the sky, set. Only sometimes did I think of it as the flaming chariot of Helios. The moon did the same, changing from phase to phase. Only sometimes did I think of it as the silver boat of Artemis. Spring, summer, fall and winter followed one another in their appointed rounds. Quite often the wind blew.

My mother-in-law, Queen Anticleia, wrinkled up like drying mud and then died, sickened by an excess of waiting, and convinced that her son would never return. My father-in-law, King Laertes, retreated to the countryside, where he was spotted shambling here and there in grubby clothing and muttering about pear trees. I suspected he was going soft in the head.

But I tried to keep up the appearance of hope, if not for myself, at least for Telemachus, who grew from year to year, indulged by all.

Penelope is in her room. Three Ithacan Maids stand by.
Penelope is singing to Telemachus, now five years old.

Daddy went to Troy.
He didn't take his darling boy.
But soon he will be back again,
With lots of slaves and golden toys –
Daddy went to Troy.

Maids (*in harmony*)
Daddy went to Troy.
He didn't take his darling boy.
But soon he will be back again,
With lots of slaves and golden toys –
Daddy went to Troy.

Eurycleia sweeps in.

Eurycleia
There you are, Telemachus, my pet! It's time for your
dinner; and then you can have a lovely bath, and a
comforting bedtime drink! Now, say goodnight to
your mother, my little woogle-poo!

Telemachus runs to Eurycleia.

Penelope
You're spoiling him.

Eurycleia
It's good for him! He'll be a king one day!

Penelope
As the twig is bent, so will the tree grow.

Eurycleia
We don't want to bend the little twiggy, do we? Oh,
nosie-nosie-no! We want him to grow straight and tall,
and get the juicy goodness out of his nice big chunk
of meat, without our crosspatch mummy making him
all sad!

Telemachus gives Penelope a smug look.

Exit all but Penelope.

Penelope
During the days I had work to do. I was now running
the kingdom all by myself. In no way had I been
prepared for such a task during my early life at
Sparta, so in the palace of Ithaca I had to learn from
scratch. But learn I did.

My policy was to build up the estates of Odysseus so
he'd have even more when he came back than he'd
had when he'd left – more sheep, more cows, more
pigs, more fields of grain, more slaves. I often dreamt
about Odysseus returning, and how I, with womanly
modesty, would reveal how well I'd done at what was
usually considered a man's business. How his face
would shine with pleasure! You're worth a thousand
Helens, he would say. Wouldn't he? And then he'd
clasp me tenderly in his arms.

We had news of how the war with Troy was going:
sometimes well, sometimes badly. Minstrels sang songs
about the notable heroes, but I waited only for news
of Odysseus. I relished those moments. There he was
making an inspiring speech, there he was uniting
quarrelling factions, there he was concocting an
astonishing falsehood. There he was disguising himself
as a runaway slave and sneaking into Troy and speaking
with Helen herself, who – the song proclaimed – had
bathed and anointed him with her very own hands.
I wasn't so fond of that part.

And then finally – after ten long years – the news
flashed from beacon to beacon – Troy had fallen.

THE FALL OF TROY

Penelope
Athene be thanked!

Eurycleia
They say it was Odysseus – he did it, just as the Oracle said he would! The walls of Troy were high and thick – no warrior could take them by force – but my Odysseus fooled those Trojans!

Ithacan Maid 1
With a wooden horse.

Ithacan Maid 2
It was hollow.

Eurycleia
He said it was an offering to the gods, but it was stuffed full of Greek soldiers . . .

Ithacan Maid 1
With swords! And spears!

Ithacan Maid 3
And the Trojans wheeled the horse inside the city walls . . .

Ithacan Maid 2
And when darkness fell . . .

An ominous humming from all the Maids, acting bloodlit chaos.

Eurycleia
The streets ran red with blood.

Ithacan Maid 1
The sky above the palace turned to fire.

Ithacan Maid 2 (*wailing*)
The Trojan women were raped.

Ithacan Maid 3
The tender young girls!

Ithacan Maid 2
Then they were shackled together – to be shipped
away as slaves.

Ithacan Maid 3
The innocent boy-children – were thrown
from a cliff! Their mangled bodies . . .

Penelope
Stop it!

The bloodlit dumbshow fades.

Ithacan Maid 1
That's what happens when you lose a war.

Eurycleia (*to Penelope*)
The Greek ships have set sail for Ithaca. He'll soon be
home now. My dear master!

SCENE 15
WAITING FOR ODYSSEUS

Penelope
Day after day I waited. I'd climb up to the top floor
of the palace and sit looking out over the harbour.
Day after day there was no sign. Sometimes there
were ships, though never the ship I longed to see. But
the ships brought rumours. And any rumour was
better than none, so I listened avidly to them all.

THE WILY SEA CAPTAIN
performed by the Maids, as Sailors.

Oh, wily Odysseus he set out from Troy,
With his boat full of loot and his heart full of joy,
For he was Athene's own shiny-eyed boy,
With his lies and his tricks and his thieving!

His first port of call was the sweet Lotus shore
Where we sailors did long to forget the foul war;
But we soon were hauled off on the black ships
    once more,
Although we were pining and grieving.

To the dread one-eyed Cyclops then next we did hie,
He wanted to eat us so we put out his eye,
Our lad said, 'I'm No One,' but then bragged, ''Twas I,
Odysseus, the prince of deceiving!'

Here's a health to our Captain, so gallant and free,
Whether stuck on a rock or asleep 'neath a tree,
Or rolled in the arms of some nymph of the sea,
Which is where we would all like to be, man!

On the island of Circe we were turned into swine,
Till Odysseus bedded the goddess so fine,
Then he ate up her cakes and he drank up her wine,
For a year he became her blithe lodger!

Although he made love till he nearly went blind,
With a goddess curvaceous and sexy and kind,
He kept sweet Penelope ever in mind,
'Tis she that does send his heart soaring!

So a health to our Captain where'er he may roam,
Tossed here and tossed there on the wide ocean's foam,
And he's in no hurry to ever get home –
Odysseus, that crafty old codger!

Penelope
And then, nothing.

Odysseus, my dear longed-for Odysseus . . . Odysseus seemed to have vanished from the face of the earth.

End of Act One.

Act Two

SCENE 16
HELEN TAKES A BATH

Hades.

A silvery laugh. Helen breezes in, with an excited, twittering procession of Suitors' and Warriors' Ghosts.

Penelope
Helen!

Helen
Oh, hello there, little cousin duck!

Penelope
Where are you off to?

Helen
I'm on my way to take my bath. Care to join me?

Penelope
We're spirits now, Helen. Spirits don't have bodies.
They don't get dirty. They have no need of baths.

Helen
Oh, but my reason for taking a bath was always
spiritual. I found it so soothing, in the midst of the
turmoil. You wouldn't have any idea of how exhausting
it is, having such vast numbers of men quarrelling over
you, year after year. Divine beauty is such a burden.
At least you've been spared that!

Penelope
Are you going to take off your spirit robes?

Helen
We're all aware of your legendary modesty, Penelope.

42

I'm sure if you ever were to bathe you'd keep your own robes on. But I do prefer to bathe without my robes, even in the spirit.

Penelope
That would explain the unusually large crowd of spectators you've attracted.

Helen
But is it unusually large? I never count them. I do feel that because so many of them died for me – well, because of me – surely I owe them something in return.

Penelope
If only a peek at what they missed on earth.

Helen
Desire does not die with the body. Only the ability to satisfy it. But a glimpse or two does perk them up, the poor lambs.

Penelope
So you're washing their blood off your hands. I hadn't realised you were capable of guilt.

Helen
Tell me, little duck – are your own hands entirely free of blood? . . .

Maids (*from the darkness*)
we are the maids
the ones you failed
the ones you killed . . .

Helen laughs.

Helen (*as she goes off*)
Goodbye, little cousin! Enjoy . . . the asphodel!

Helen leaves. The Suitors' Ghosts follow her, looking back reproachfully at Penelope.

SCENE 17
THE SUITORS STUFF THEIR FACES

Penelope

By this stage there was an increasing amount of
curiosity about me, as there was bound to be about the
wife – or was it the widow? – of such a famous man;
if Odysseus were proved to have died, might I be open
to other offers?

The suitors did not appear on the scene right away.
For the first nine or ten years of Odysseus' absence we
knew where he was – he was at Troy – and we knew
he was still alive. So the suitors waited. They waited
until hope had dwindled and was flickering out.

*The Suitors start arriving in their droves. By the end
of her speech, Penelope is surrounded.*

First five came, then ten, then fifty – the more there
were, the more were attracted, each fearing to miss
out on the perpetual feasting and the marriage lottery.
They were like vultures when they spot a dead cow:
one drops, then another, until finally every vulture for
miles around is tearing up the carcass.

She tries to move away.

Excuse me, gentlemen.

Wherever she turns, a Suitor stands in her way.

Suitor 1

Fair Penelope!

Suitor 2

Beauteous Penelope! My knees melt at the sight of
you!

Suitor 3

Penelope of the divine form, kindest and most sagacious of all women! Take pity on me!

Suitor 4

Queen Penelope! Royal widow! You owe it to suffering mankind to choose a new king for your consort, and put us out of our miserable suspense.

Penelope

But Odysseus is alive! An oracle has said so.

Suitor 1

The sea teems with marauding pirates. They're fond of attacking palaces.

Suitor 3

Looting. Stealing. Carrying women off as slaves.

Suitor 2

It's not safe for a queen here all alone – a rich queen, such as yourself – without a king to protect her.

Suitor 3

Her, and her son.

Suitor 1

You wouldn't want anything to happen to *him*!

Penelope hurries out.

Telemachus, now a teenager on the verge of manhood, enters. He's displeased.

Here comes the little snot now.

Suitor 2

Acts like he owns the place.

The Suitors mock Telemachus with a reprise of Penelope's lullaby.

Suitors
> Daddy went to Troy.
> He didn't take his darling boy.
> He's never coming back again!
> *We'll* get your slaves and golden toys –
> Daddy went to Troy!

> *They laugh.*

Telemachus
> He *is* coming back! Then you'll be sorry! He'll – he'll
> shoot you full of arrows!

Suitor 1
> Then we'll be sorry! (*He laughs.*)

Suitor 2
> Who's gonna make us?

Suitor 3
> Not you, you snivelling little mama's boy!

> *Telemachus, humiliated, hurries out.*

Suitor 2 (*claps his hands*)
> Maids! Slaves!

> *Enter two Maids. One of the Suitors pinches a bum.*

Suitor 3
> Bring me a lamb. I'll slaughter it myself.

Suitor 4
> I want beef. Bring me a cow.

Suitor 2
> A goat for me!

Suitor 1
> I want a pig!

Suitor 5
> Wine! Bring wine!

Suitor 2

First we'll roast, then we'll feast! Heap up the platters!

A slaughtering scene goes on during this, in which the animals getting their throats cut are played by Maids.

The Suitors eat like pigs.

Suitor 3

Keep stuffing it in, lads! At this rate there'll be nothing left, and then Queen Penelope will have to make a decision!

Suitor 1

A toast to Penelope . . . 'Marry or starve!'

Suitors

Marry or starve!

They clink glasses and drink.

Suitor 1

First prize, a week in Penelope's bed, second prize, two weeks in Penelope's bed.

They laugh.

Suitor 2

Close your eyes and they're all the same – just imagine she's Helen, that'll put bronze in your spear!

Suitor 3

When's the old bitch going to make up her mind? Let's murder the son, get him out of the way while he's young – the little bastard's starting to get on my nerves.

Suitor 4

What's to stop one of us from just grabbing the old cow and making off with her?

Suitor 2

No, lads, that would be cheating. You know our bargain – whoever gets the prize gives out respectable gifts to the others, we're agreed, right? We're all in this together, do or die.

Suitor 3

You do, she dies, because whoever wins has to fuck her to death!

SCENE 18
PENELOPE GETS AN IDEA

Hades.

Penelope

Month by month the pressure on me increased. What could I do to stop these aristocratic young thugs? They were at the age when they were all swagger, so appeals to their generosity, attempts to reason with them and threats of retribution alike had no effect. Complaining to their parents did no good: their families stood to gain by their behaviour. And the men who might have been loyal to Odysseus had sailed off with him to Troy.

Eurycleia was especially diligent in the reporting of malicious gossip, whether true or invented: most probably she was trying to harden my heart against the suitors and their ardent pleas, so I would remain faithful to the very last gasp. She was always Odysseus' biggest fan.

Telemachus was growing up, and he was starting to look at me in an odd way. He knew that if I stayed in Ithaca and married one of the suitors, that suitor would become the king, and his stepfather, and being

48

ordered around by a lad not much older than himself did not appeal.

I knew it would do no good to try to expel my unwanted suitors, or to bar the palace doors against them. If I tried that, they'd turn really ugly and go on the rampage and snatch by force what they were attempting to win by persuasion. But I was the daughter of a Naiad. *Behave like water*, I told myself. *Don't try to oppose them. When they try to grasp you, slip through their fingers. Flow around them.*

For this reason I pretended to view their wooing favourably, encouraging one, then another, and even sending them secret messages.

Finally, a scheme occurred to me.

SCENE 19
THE SHROUD

The courtyard. Penelope addresses her Suitors.

Penelope
I come to reassure you that your waiting is nearly over. Last night the ghost of Odysseus appeared to me in a dream. I accept the sad fact that he is no longer among the living. His soul has fluttered down to Hades, and he roams the fields of asphodel, with all the other fallen heroes.

The Suitors jostle for position. Several fall on their knees, and hold out their hands to her.

Suitors
Choose me! Me! Choose me!

Penelope
But I have one task I must complete before I select

a husband. My father-in-law, Laertes, is an old man. It would be impious of me not to provide a costly winding sheet for him when he dies, so I must weave a royal shroud for him, or incur the gods' anger.

The Suitors are disappointed, but they see the logic of what she's saying.

When this sacred work is finished, I will speedily nominate a husband. Choosing will be difficult, since you all have so many extraordinary qualities. But choose I shall.

The Suitors murmur in agreement.

Suitor 1
Fairest Penelope, we respect your pious and dutiful intention, and we will wait – although impatiently, and burning with desire – until its completion, when one of us will be made the happiest man on earth!

Penelope
I recruited twelve of my favourite maidservants, the youngest and most beautiful. They'd been with me all their lives, born of slaves in the palace; I'd brought them up myself, as playmates for Telemachus, and trained them carefully in everything:

Melantho; Tanis; Kerthia; Iole; Celandine; Klytie; Selene; Zoe; Alecto; Chloris; Phasiana; Narcissa.

The Maids – the Twelve Favoured Maids – bring in a loom, formed by each one of them holding a rope; they do a twining dance, as Penelope weaves.

Maids
(*singing softly as background while they weave in and out*)

Weaving, weaving, ever grieving,
While the trees are bending, sighing,

Sadly twining, ever pining,
Weave a shroud for royal bones . . .

Weaving, grieving, interwinding,
While the waves are rising, falling,
Twisting, turning, ever yearning
For the one who's gone from home . . .

Poor, the Queen without a King here,
While the time goes passing slowly,
Softly praying, daily mourning,
Prisoned in her royal home . . .

As the Maids sing and form a fabric, the Suitors look on, as does Telemachus.

Penelope
Alas! This shroud would be a fitter garment for me than for King Laertes, wretched that I am, and doomed by the gods to a life that is a living death. Oh, how I pray for this task to end so I am free to marry again and please a living man!

She looks longingly at her Suitors and pretends to cry.

Telemachus (*under his breath*)
Shame on you, faithless mother.

Suitor 1
Most diligent Penelope, we will retire so that you may weave ever more quickly – and so our hearts will not break with longing for you!

Telemachus and the Suitors leave.

Night falls. The fabric of ropes glows in the dark.
Penelope sits up in her chair, and the Maids tiptoe in,
giggling softly.

Melantho
Good evening, ma'am.

Penelope
Call me Penelope – let's dispense with formalities.
We're amongst friends. Come, sit down!

Kerthia
I brought us some figs.

Penelope
My favourite!

Tanis
And some bread dipped in honeycomb.

Iole (*a little over-excited*)
A midnight feast!

Klytie
I've brought some wine.

Penelope
Lock the door . . . no one must know we're here.

Together they start unpicking the shroud. The Maids
sing quietly: a round.

Maids
Weaving, grieving, out and in,
While our tangled web we spin.
Moon's above, and gone the sun,
Pick the threads out one by one;

Weaving, grieving, all deceiving,
Night undoes what day has done;
Weaving, grieving, out and in,
Night and secrecy help us win,
Never we'll finish what we've begun!
When will dear Odysseus come?

*The fabric of ropes comes apart as they sing and move
out and in.*

Penelope
That's enough for one night. What news of the
suitors?

Kerthia
The fat one is getting impatient.

Melantho
Antinous?

Kerthia
Maybe he suspects something.

Penelope
Melantho . . . I need you to distract him.

Melantho
But how, ma'am?

Penelope
You'll think of something. Stick close to the suitors –
that way we'll always know their plans. You can even
say rude and disrespectful things about me, or
Telemachus, or even Odysseus himself – that will
make the illusion more convincing.

Melantho (*practising*)
Queen Penelope is a very clumsy weaver!

Penelope smiles.

Penelope

I'm so proud of you girls. You're my most trusted eyes and ears. When Odysseus gets home he'll be so very, very pleased with you all.

The Maids look flattered.

For more than three years we picked away at my weaving at the dead of night. And though we were permanently exhausted, these nights had a touch of festivity amongst them. They were such pleasant girls, full of energy; a little loud and giggly sometimes, as all maids are in youth, but it cheered me up to hear them chattering away, and to listen to their singing. They had such lovely voices, all of them. We told stories as we worked away at our task of destruction; we shared riddles; we made jokes. We became like sisters.

And in the mornings, our eyes darkened by lack of sleep, we'd exchange smiles of complicity, and here and there a quick squeeze of the hand. Their 'Yes ma'ams' and 'No ma'ams' hovered on the edge of laughter, as if neither they nor I could take their servile behaviour seriously.

In retrospect, I can see that my actions were ill-considered, and caused harm. But I was running out of time, and becoming desperate, and I had to use every ruse and stratagem at my command.

SCENE 21
THE UNPLEASANT BANQUET

The Maids are flirting with the Suitors. Melantho is paying special attention to Antinous. His hands keep wandering; she keeps pushing them away.

Telemachus eyes the Maids and the Suitors with disgust.

54

Telemachus
Mother! Why don't you put a stop to this? They're disgusting!

Penelope
Your father isn't here. And what can I do? Now I must get back to my weaving.

She takes her leave, and gives a nod and a smile to Melantho. Melantho nods back.

Antinous eyes this exchange suspiciously.

Telemachus
Sluts and bloodsuckers, all of you. Just wait till my father gets home!

Telemachus follows Penelope out, fuming.

Melantho
What was that about?

Antinous
What do you mean?

Antinous
She looked at you funny.

Melantho
The old bat's got a wall eye, that's all.

Antinous (*to the room at large*)
I saw it. She looked at you funny.

The other Suitors pay attention.

She's taking a long time with that stupid shroud of hers! Right, boys?

Suitors
Right!

Melantho
Queen Penelope is a very clumsy weaver!

Antinous
What's she really up to?

Melantho
Nothing!

Antinous
I'm going to follow her.

Melantho
No! (*Flirting.*) I mean – don't leave me all by myself.
I'll get lonely!

Antinous grabs Melantho roughly. She tries to get away.

Antinous
Melantho of the Pretty Cheeks! Not so fast!

Melantho
Let go of me!

Antinous
Off to help your mistress?

He pushes her down. She screams.

Suitors
Fair shares for all!

Several more Suitors pile onto Melantho. They rape her. Other Suitors grab other Maids.

SCENE 22
CHORUS: DREAMBOATS, A BALLAD

Maids

Sleep is the only rest we get;
It's then we are at peace:
We do not have to mop the floor
And wipe away the grease.

We are not chased around the hall
And tumbled in the dirt
By every greedy thug and lout
Who wants a slice of skirt.

And when we sleep we like to dream;
We dream we are at sea,
We sail the waves in golden boats,
So happy, clean and free.

In dreams we all are beautiful
In glossy crimson dresses;
We sleep with every man we love,
We shower them with kisses.

They fill our days with feasting,
We fill their nights with song,
We take them in our golden boats
And drift the whole year long.

And all is mirth and kindness,
There are no tears of pain;
For our decrees are merciful
Throughout our golden reign.

But then the morning wakes us up:
Once more we toil and slave,
And hoist our skirts at their command
For every prick and knave.

57

SCENE 23
BAD NEWS

*Eurycleia and Penelope are tending to the bruises of
Melantho and the other Maids.*

Eurycleia
Well, what could you expect? Hanging around them
like that. Tempting them. It's outrageous! Queen
Penelope, you spoil these girls, you really do. You
should hear what they say about you behind your back.
They're all in cahoots with the suitors. They deserve
a good whipping! That's what Odysseus would do!

Penelope
Eurycleia. We need more water.

Eurycleia
Yes, my lady.

She bustles out.

Melantho
Queen Penelope, you must tell her! Tell her it was by
your orders. She hates us!

Penelope
It's too dangerous. She's a terrible gossip – the suitors
will find out! Try to stand it until your master comes
back . . .

Eurycleia (*hurries in*)
My lady! Bad news!

Penelope
What? Tell me! Is Odysseus . . .

Eurycleia
Telemachus has taken one of the boats and has gone
off in search of his father.

Penelope
Oh – but he's too young – he's never sailed a boat!
My poor boy! Now he'll die, and I'll be completely
alone . . . (*Beat.*) But he must have taken a boatload of
supplies . . . How did he get the key to the storeroom?
Eurycleia! Tell me the truth! You helped him!

Eurycleia
Oh dear . . . how could I refuse him? He made me
promise not to tell you, because he didn't want you to
fret! He's so headstrong – he's at the age when a young
man needs to assert himself – just as my darling
Odysseus did!

Penelope
He's not as cunning as Odysseus.

Eurycleia
Oh, my lady – I didn't think of that! And now there's
worse –

Penelope
Worse?

Eurycleia
I've heard that the suitors are planning to ambush him
and murder him on his return.

Penelope
Athene give me strength!

Eurycleia
Now, my lady, never you mind . . . It will turn out
well – because the gods are just, and they don't want
you to suffer! Now I'll make you a lovely comforting
bedtime drink!

She bustles out.

SCENE 24
TELEMACHUS RETURNS

Penelope

I didn't believe that the gods did not want me to
suffer. They all tease. I might as well have been a stray
dog pelted with stones or with its tail set alight for
their amusement. Not the fat and bones of animals,
but our human suffering, is what they like to savour.

Sometimes, however, they relent.

Telemachus enters.

Telemachus! Thank the gods! You're safe!

She hugs him. Penelope pulls away, shakes him.

What were you thinking? You've got the brains of a
newt! You're barely more than a child! You have no
experience at commanding a ship! You could have
been killed fifty times over, and then what would your
father say?

Telemachus

I'm not a child any longer, I'm a man! I know what
I'm doing – I got back all right, didn't I?

Penelope

More by good luck than good judgement! How dare
you go off like that, without even asking permission?

Telemachus

I don't need your permission to take a boat that more
or less belongs to me. It's part of my inheritance,
though no thanks to you that I have any inheritance
left! Those suitors of yours are eating it all up – with
a lot of help from those slutty maids!

Penelope
What on earth can I do? I have no control over them.
You see how things are.

Telemachus
Someone in this family has got to show some backbone!
My father would be proud of me for having the guts
to go out and look for him – away from this pigsty
and all the weak-minded women who live in it.

Penelope
How could you refer to your own mother as 'the
women'?

Telemachus (*rolling his eyes*)
Here it comes. 'You've-no-idea-what-I've-been-through-
for-your-sake-no-woman-should-have-to-put-up-with-
this-kind-of-suffering-I-might-as-well-kill-myself.'

Penelope starts to cry.

Eurycleia! Eurycleia! Hurry up!

Eurycleia (*bustles in*)
Telemachus! Dear child! You're back!

Telemachus
Get one of the maids to run me a bath. I'm tired. And
I'm starving too. Bring me some food!

*The Maids bring in platters of food, which Telemachus
starts to gobble.*

Penelope
Telemachus! Manners!

Telemachus (*mouth full*)
Manners are for girls.

A Maid rubs his shoulders while he eats.

Penelope

So did you discover anything about Odysseus on your little jaunt? And if you did, could you possibly bear to share it with me?

Telemachus

Why would you care?

Penelope

I'm his wife.

Silence.

Was there even the smallest . . . was there a hint – was there *any* news of Odysseus?

Telemachus (*self-important*)

According to Menelaus . . .

Penelope

You saw Menelaus?

Telemachus

According to Menelaus, my father is alive and well . . .

Penelope

The gods be praised!

Telemachus

But he can't get away. He's trapped on a tropical island . . .

Penelope

With a beautiful goddess who makes love to him night after night. Yes, I've heard those rumours before.

Telemachus

And, of course, I saw Helen.

Penelope

Oh. Yes. Helen.

Telemachus
She gave us a *great* dinner!

Penelope
And how did Helen . . . look?

Telemachus
As radiant as golden Aphrodite! It was a real thrill to see her. She was everything she's cracked up to be!

Penelope
She must be getting a little *older*, by now, surely?

Telemachus
Not that you could tell, no.

Penelope smiles, and looks away to hide her disappointment. There's a silence.

Penelope
Well, anyway, I'm glad the suitors didn't murder you.

Telemachus (*softening*)
Actually, Helen did look quite old. Way older than you. Sort of worn out. All wrinkly. Like an old mushroom. And her teeth are yellow. Actually some of them have fallen out. It was only after I'd had a lot to drink that she looked beautiful.

Penelope (*pleased*)
Thank you, my son. Goodnight.

SCENE 25
SURPRISED IN THE NIGHT

Darkness. The shroud fabric drops down, bigger now. The Maids (all but Melantho) and Penelope unweave part of the fabric.

63

Maids (*singing, but more sadly than before*)
 Weaving, grieving, out and in,
 While our tangled web we spin.
 Moon's above, and gone the sun,
 Pick the threads out one by one;
 Weaving, grieving, all deceiving,
 Night undoes what day has done;
 Weaving, grieving, out and in,
 Night and secrecy help us win,
 Deepest midnight, moon's above,
 So we work our task of love;
 Never we'll finish what we've begun!
 When will dear Odysseus come?
 When oh when oh when oh when –
 When will dear Odysseus come?

Penelope
 My dearest girls. I'm so sorry. They're pigs – all of
 them.

 The Maids don't look up.

 When Odysseus comes back, I'll make sure he knows
 everything. I'll tell him the whole story of your loyalty
 to me and you'll be rewarded. I'll tell him how you've
 helped me. I'll tell him you've been like daughters to
 me.

 *The Suitors hammer at the door. The door bursts open
 and they rush in, hauling Melantho with them.*

Suitor 1
 We've caught you now!

Suitor 2
 Thought you were so clever!

Suitor 3
 You lied! You cheated! You deceived us!

64

Suitor 1 (*threatening with a sword*)
  Now – you – must – *choose*!

SCENE 26
BAD DREAMS

Sunset.

Penelope
  Now began the worst period of my ordeal. I cried so
  much I thought I would turn into a river or a fountain,
  as in the old tales.

  O Pallas Athene, goddess of ingenuity and friend of
  Odysseus, despair overwhelms me! I beg you on my
  knees – I implore you – show me a plan to defeat the
  suitors, or send me a sign that Odysseus is on his way
  back to my adoring arms!

  But still Odysseus did not come. The gods kept me in
  suspense. I think they pull a lot of their pranks because
  they're bored. 'Which prayer shall we answer today?'
  they ask one another. 'Let's cast dice! Hope here,
  despair there, and let's destroy the life of that woman
  down there by having sex with her in the form of a
  crayfish!' Not the fat and bones of sacrificed animals,
  but our human suffering, is what the gods love to
  savour.

  That is what I often thought, in my darker moments.

  Eurycleia bustles in with a cup.

Eurycleia
  Here's your comforting bedtime drink, my child. Try
  to sleep.

Penelope
  When I sleep, I have bad dreams.

65

Eurycleia

There, there, my child. You worry too much! Drink this, and may the gods send you better visions!

She leaves. Penelope drinks, and lies down. A sequence of bad dreams begins.

Naiad Mother

Remember, water does not resist. Water always goes where it wants to go, and nothing in the end can stand against it. Water is patient. Dripping water wears away a stone. Remember, my child – you are half water. If you can't go through an obstacle, go around it. Water does.

The Maids come one by one, as dreams, dressed as sailors. The Maids sing.

Maid

Oh, wily Odysseus, he set out from Troy,
With his boat full of loot and his heart full of joy,
For he was Athene's own shiny-eyed boy,
With his lies and his tricks and his thieving!

To the Isle of the Dead then Odysseus did stray,
Filled a trench up with blood, held the spirits at bay,
Till he learned what Teiresias the seer had to say,
Odysseus, the artfullest dodger!

Three Maids

The Sirens' sweet singing then next he did brave,
They attempted to lure him to a feathery grave,
While tied to the mast he did rant and did rave,
But Odysseus alone learned their riddle!

Maid

The whirlpool Charybdis did not our lad catch,
Nor snake-headed Scylla, she could not him snatch,
Then he ran the fell rocks that would grind you to
    scratch,
For their clashing he gave not a piddle!

Maid

We men did a bad turn against his command,
When we ate the Sun's cattle, they sure tasted grand,
In a storm we all perished, but our Captain reached
    land,
On the isle of the goddess Calypso.

Maid

After seven long years there of kissing and woo,
He escaped on a raft that was drove to and fro,
Till fair Nausicaa's maids that the laundry did do,
Found him bare on the beach – he did drip so!

Maid

Then he told his adventures and laid to his store
A hundred disasters and sufferings galore,
For no one can tell what the Fates have in store,
Not Odysseus, that master disguiser.

Three Maids

So a health to our Captain, where'er he may be,
Whether walking the earth or adrift on the sea,
For he's not down in Hades, unlike all of we –
And we leave you not any the wiser!

Daylight. Penelope wakes up.

Penelope

Who is to say that prayers have any effect? On the
other hand, who is to say they don't? Twenty years of
my prayers had gone unanswered. But, finally, not this
one. No sooner had I performed the familiar shedding
of tears than Odysseus himself shambled into the
courtyard.

SCENE 27
THE DIRTY OLD BEGGAR

The courtyard. Maids are hauling buckets around, mopping, etc. Odysseus shambles in, disguised.

Odysseus
Is this the palace of the renowned Odysseus, of Trojan horse fame, master of deceiving tricks, and well-known for his hospitality to strangers?

Tanis
Who wants to know?

Telemachus has entered, and is listening.

Odysseus
A worthy aristocrat, whom the Fates have deprived of his rightful inheritance, now driven to travel the seas as an outcast.

Melantho
You look more like a dirty old beggar to me. You should piss off out of here before one of the Queen's suitors sees you. They'll beat you up!

Telemachus
And you'll help them, you faithless whores!

The Maids scurry off.

(*To Odysseus.*) Sir – in your travels – have you heard any news of my father, Odysseus?

Odysseus (*restraining himself*)
Odysseus was your father? You're Prince Telemachus?

Telemachus nods.

Then I can tell you – Odysseus is alive.

Antinous swaggers on, scratching himself. There are two other Suitors with him.

Antinous

Alive? Him? Not likely! I hope he's rotting in Hades. (*Pushing Odysseus.*) Now sod off, you dumb shit! If you're here when I get back, I'll bash your brains in! (*To Telemachus.*) As for you, pipsqueak – run off to your mummy!

The Suitors stroll off together, laughing and singing:

Daddy went to Troy,
He didn't take his darling boy –
He's never coming back again!
We'll get the slaves and golden toys,
Daddy went to Troy . . .

Telemachus (*calling after them*)

You'll be singing another tune when Odysseus comes back!

Odysseus

My son. I am back.

Telemachus

What?

Odysseus

I'm your father.

They embrace.

Telemachus

But . . . you look so . . .

Penelope appears. Eurycleia behind her.

Odysseus (*aside*)

It's a disguise! Don't tell your mother. She'll give me away! I need your help. Quick – go and count the weapons in the storeroom.

Telemachus runs off.

Penelope
Sir, I am not fully mistress in my own home, but I can still respect the laws of hospitality. (*To Eurycleia.*) We will dine together.

Eurycleia
But, dear child, he's only a dirty old . . .

Penelope
Do as I say.

Penelope and Odysseus sit on stools. During their conversation, Eurycleia brings food.

Odysseus
Admired Queen, the songs tell of your faithfulness towards your absent husband, of your many trials, and of your clever trick with the shroud. What will you do now?

Penelope
I intend to tell the suitors that I'll marry whoever among them can string the great bow of Odysseus, and fire an arrow through twelve round axe-heads.

Odysseus
Are they skilled enough to do that?

Penelope
Only Odysseus himself could perform such a feat.

Odysseus
Then it's a good plan. Odysseus will approve.

Penelope gazes at him.

Penelope
You truly believe he's still alive?

Odysseus
I know it.

Penelope
Oh Sir – you give me hope! I've been so alone, all these years. And I've had such bad dreams.

Odysseus
Every dream is a hidden door.

Penelope
A door into the heart?

Odysseus
Yes.

Penelope
And you can always open it?

Odysseus nods, but says nothing.

Penelope
I dream I have a flock of beautiful, lovely white geese, geese of which I am very, very fond. I dream that they are happily pecking around the yard when a huge eagle with a crooked beak swoops down and kills them all. And then I wake up in tears.

Odysseus
The eagle is your husband, Odysseus, who will soon return and slay the suitors.

Penelope
But if the geese are the suitors, why do their deaths make me sad?

Eurycleia (*entering*)
My lady. It's very late.

Penelope

Yes. Make up the best fleece bed for our visitor, and wash his feet.

Eurycleia

His feet? (*Whispering.*) But madam – they're so dirty!

Penelope

All the more reason to wash them.

Eurycleia grumbles, bringing water.

Odysseus

I'm pleased you've chosen an old slave for this task, rather than a young and beautiful one, who would scorn my poor battered feet. These feet have travelled many weary miles . . .

Eurycleia (*barely concealing her disgust*)

Many was the time I washed the feet of my dear master, Odysseus. That was over twenty years ago now. I'd recognise those feet anywhere. All firm and shapely, they were. And he had a long scar on his thigh. Made by a wild boar. Right about here.

She sees the scar. Penelope turns away as Eurycleia yelps in shock and overturns the basin of water.

Oh, sweet master!

Odysseus grabs her by the throat.

Odysseus

One word and you're dead!

Penelope (*aside*)

May the gods forgive me for this little joke I played on Eurycleia. Of course I'd recognised Odysseus at once – how could I have mistaken those short legs? But I didn't let on, because it's always an imprudence to step between a man and the reflection of his own cleverness.

(*To them.*) Till tomorrow – when I'll bring out the great bow of Odysseus.

Eurycleia
I'll fetch your bedtime drink, my lady.

Penelope goes out.

Odysseus
Make sure she sleeps very soundly. And lock her into the women's quarters. She's too tender-hearted for bloodshed.

Eurycleia nods. Penelope gets into her bed.

Penelope
Tomorrow I'd be able to tell my twelve maids who he really was. In the meantime, I knew they'd faithfully continue their rudeness to Telemachus, and join the suitors in their insults. What a joy it would be to me when at last I could tell Odysseus that my girls had been acting in his interests all along!

Eurycleia brings her a drink, in a very large cup. Penelope sleeps. Eurycleia locks the door.

SCENE 28
THE SLAUGHTER IN THE HALL

Morning. Eurycleia sets up the huge bow. The Suitors meanwhile have gathered, and are warming up.

Telemachus watches from the sidelines.

Eurycleia
Behold – the great bow of Odysseus.

Antinous
Hmph. Doesn't look like much.

73

Eurycleia

Honoured sirs – contestants for the hand of Queen Penelope – who will make the first attempt?

Antinous

This'll be easy.

He fails to string the bow. Others try. Grumbling. No success.

Odysseus

May I try?

Antinous

You? Don't insult us, you mangy scum.

Suitor 2

Oh let him do it! Good for a laugh anyway!

Odysseus steps up, strings the bow. Grunts of amazement from the Suitors.

Odysseus

Now – an arrow through all twelve axe-heads.

They watch the arrow fly. Success!

Antinous

That's not possible! Only Odysseus could ever do that! The old fart must have cheated!

Odysseus pulls the bowstring back again, lets fly an arrow. Antinous clutches his throat, falls down. Mayhem. Odysseus throws off his cloak, revealing armour.

Suitor 2 (*in terror*)

Odysseus!

Odysseus

Yes! Odysseus! Now we'll see who's master in this house!

Suitors
    Kill him!

Blood-red mime scene of Odysseus shooting arrow after arrow as the Suitors charge him, fall back, fall down. Telemachus too has entered the fray, with a sword and spears. The Suitors are all felled. Odysseus and Telemachus embrace.

Odysseus
    Eurycleia! Bring the maids here. Have them haul the bodies out and then wash the blood and brains off the floor. The palace must be cleansed.

The Maids crawl around on the floor, wailing and scrubbing.

Eurycleia
    And then?

Odysseus
    Kill them. They've been dishonoured. I know what was going on between them and the suitors. I can't have such pollution in my palace.

Telemachus
    Not all of them, Father!

Odysseus (*tired*)
    Which ones, then?

Eurycleia
    Twelve of them. The youngest ones. The disloyal ones. The impertinent ones. The prettiest ones.

The Maids listen, horrified.

Odysseus
    As you wish. I'm going to wash off this blood. Telemachus – see it done.

He exits.

Maids (*beseeching Telemachus*)
No, young master! Call the Queen! She'll tell you – we were only helping her! We were following her orders!

Telemachus (*confused, to Eurycleia*)
What do they mean? I don't understand.

Eurycleia
Pay no attention to them, dear master. They'll say anything to save themselves!

Telemachus
Maybe I should wait until . . .

Eurycleia
Do as your father says.

Nooses drop down from above. The Maids are hanged.

SCENE 29
THE SAD AWAKENING

Eurycleia shakes Penelope awake.

Eurycleia
Come quickly, my child.

Penelope
Eurycleia? What is it? (*She sees the blood on Eurycleia's clothes.*) What's happened?

Eurycleia
Odysseus. Dear, sweet Odysseus. He's home at last. And he's slain all the suitors! (*She claps her hands in delight.*)

Penelope

The gods be thanked! But when? What time is it? Where are my twelve maids? I must tell them the news – at last their ordeal is over! And Odysseus. I must explain everything to Odysseus. How happy . . .

Eurycleia

The maids have been hanged, my lady.

Penelope

What?

Eurycleia

Not all of them.

Penelope

But which maids? Dear gods – which maids did they hang?

Eurycleia

Mistress, dear child. He wanted to kill them all! I had to choose some – otherwise all would have perished!

Penelope

Which ones?

Eurycleia

Only . . . twelve.

Penelope

Twelve?

Eurycleia

The ones who'd been rude. The ones who used to thumb their noses at me. Melantho of the Pretty Cheeks and her cronies – that lot. They were notorious whores.

Penelope

The ones who'd been raped. The youngest. The most beautiful. (*To herself.*) My eyes and ears among the

77

suitors. My helpers during the long nights of the
shroud. My snow-white geese. My thrushes, my doves.

Eurycleia

The suitors fancied them. They let it go to their heads.
It wouldn't have done for King Odysseus to allow
such tarnished girls to continue to serve in the palace.
He could never have trusted them. Now come, dear
child. Your husband is waiting to see you.

SCENE 30
THE INVOCATION OF THE FURIES

Hades.

*Whispering. Bat squeakings. Asphodel. The Maids are
blood-dyed.*

Maids

We demand justice!

We demand retribution!

We invoke the law of blood guilt!

We call upon the Angry Ones!

O Angry Ones, O Furies, you are our last hope!

We implore you to inflict punishment and exact
vengeance on our behalf!

Be our defenders, we who had none in life!

Smell out Odysseus wherever he goes!

From one place to another, from one life to another!

Whatever disguise he puts on,

Whatever shape he may take,

Hunt him down!

Dog his footsteps.

On earth or in Hades.

Wherever he may take refuge!

Appear to him in our forms.

Our ruined forms!

The forms of our pitiable corpses.

Let him never be at rest!

SCENE 31
THE BED OF MANY SECRETS

Penelope is sitting on her bed.

Odysseus enters quietly, now in clean clothing. They look at each other.

Penelope
Twenty years ago, my beloved husband told me many wonderful stories in this very bed.

Odysseus
Now I have many more to tell you.

Beat.

Penelope
You'll find our bed exactly as you left it.

Odysseus
Whittled from an olive tree that had its living roots still in the ground, so no one would ever be able to move it.

Penelope

That was our secret. No one else knew.

So it really is you, then.

Odysseus

I'm not the young man I once was.

Penelope

Nor I the same young girl.

Odysseus

So much time gone. So much blood spilled.

Penelope wipes a tear.

No need to cry. I'm home now.

Penelope

And so we climbed into the very same bed where we had spent so many happy hours when we were first married. I'm glad it was dark by then, as in the shadows we both appeared less wizened than we were.

But I couldn't hold back my tears. Odysseus believed they were all for him. He told me how much he'd missed me, and how he'd been filled with longing for me even when enfolded in the white arms of immortal goddesses; and I told him how very many tears I'd shed while waiting twenty years for his return, and how tediously faithful I'd been, and how I would never have even so much as thought of betraying his gigantic bed with its enormous bedpost by sleeping in it with any other man.

The two of us were now proficient and shameless liars of long standing. It's a wonder either one of us believed a word the other said.

But we did.

Or so we told each other.

SCENE 32
HOME LIFE IN HADES

Hades.

Penelope

I suppose you know the rules. If we wish to, we can get ourselves reborn, and have another try at life; though first we have to drink from the Waters of Forgetfulness, so our past lives will be wiped from our memories. But who's to say my next life wouldn't be worse? Even from here I can see that the world is just as dangerous as it was in my day – misery and suffering have not disappeared. If anything, they're even worse.

None of this stops Odysseus. He'll drop in down here for a while, he'll act pleased to see me, he'll tell me home life with me was the only thing he ever really wanted. We'll take a peaceful stroll, snack on some asphodel, tell the old stories; and then, just when I'm starting to relax, when I'm feeling that I can forgive him for everything he put me through and accept him with all his faults, when I'm starting to believe that this time he really means it, off he goes again, making a beeline for the River Lethe to be born again, and to have more life-threatening adventures.

He does mean what he tells me. He really does. He wants to be with me. He weeps when he says it. But then some force tears us apart.

The Maids appear. They have ropes around their necks.

It's the maids. He sees them in the distance, heading our way. They make him nervous. They cause him pain. They make him want to be anywhere and anyone else.

(*To the Maids.*) Why can't you leave him alone? Hasn't he done enough? He atoned for the blood, he said the prayers, he got himself purified! What more do you want from him? What do you want from *me*? Just tell me!

The Maids titter eerily, bat-like, and circle away from her.

Maids

we had no voice
we had no name
we had no choice
we had one face
one face the same

we took the blame
it was not fair
but now we're here
we're all here too
the same as you

and now we follow
you, we find you
now, we call
to you to you
too wit too woo
too wit too woo
too woo

Penelope

They never talk to me, down here. They never stay. I hold out my arms to them, my doves, my loveliest ones. But they only run away.

Run isn't quite accurate. Their legs don't move. Their still-twitching feet don't touch the ground.

The Maids dance away in a line, with their ropes around their necks, singing.

The End.